PRINCEWILL LAGANG

Building a Christ-Centered Marriage: A Blueprint for Love

First published by PRINCEWILL LAGANG 2023

Copyright © 2023 by Princewill Lagang

All rights reserved. No part of this publication may be reproduced, stored or transmitted in any form or by any means, electronic, mechanical, photocopying, recording, scanning, or otherwise without written permission from the publisher. It is illegal to copy this book, post it to a website, or distribute it by any other means without permission.

Princewill Lagang asserts the moral right to be identified as the author of this work.

First edition

This book was professionally typeset on Reedsy. Find out more at reedsy.com

Contents

1	The Foundation of Love	1
2	The Cornerstone of Faith	4
3	Love in Action	7
4	A Shared Purpose	10
5	Nurturing the Garden of Love	13
6	Weathering Life's Storms	16
7	An Ever-Deepening Love	19
8	A Legacy of Love	22
9	Embracing the Journey	25
10	A Legacy of Love Continues	28
11	Passing the Torch of Faith and Love	31
12	The Ongoing Story of Love	34

1

The Foundation of Love

Title: Building a Christ-Centered Marriage: A Blueprint for Love

It was a warm summer day when Emily and Michael exchanged their vows before God and their loved ones, committing to a lifetime of love, partnership, and faith. Their journey into building a Christ-centered marriage began with a profound sense of purpose and an unwavering belief that their love could weather any storm. As they walked down the aisle hand in hand, they were taking the first steps toward a lifelong journey of devotion and unity.

The Setting

The sun cast a golden glow over the quaint, little church where Emily and Michael celebrated their wedding. Their journey had started long before the day they tied the knot, a journey filled with shared dreams, laughter, and the occasional tear. They knew that a strong marriage would require more than just the promises spoken on this beautiful day; it would require effort, faith, and a blueprint built on the teachings of Christ.

The Promise

The essence of a Christ-centered marriage lies in the commitment to follow in the footsteps of Christ, who is the ultimate example of love and sacrifice. As Emily and Michael stood at the altar, they made a covenant not just with each other but with their Savior. They vowed to build a love that would stand the test of time, anchored in their shared faith and unwavering devotion to the teachings of Christ.

The Blueprint for Love

The blueprint for a Christ-centered marriage is a roadmap that guides couples in nurturing a love that reflects the love of Christ. It provides the necessary structure for building a strong foundation on which a lifetime of love and happiness can be constructed. As Emily and Michael embarked on this journey, they knew that their blueprint was founded on three fundamental pillars:

1. Faith in Christ

At the heart of a Christ-centered marriage is an unshakable faith in Christ. Emily and Michael understood that their love was not solely about their connection to each other but also their connection to God. They committed to seeking His guidance in every aspect of their marriage and allowing His love to permeate every facet of their lives.

2. Selfless Love

In Corinthians 13:4-7, the Bible beautifully defines the nature of love: "Love is patient, love is kind. It does not envy, it does not boast, it is not proud. It does not dishonor others, it is not self-seeking, it is not easily angered, it keeps no record of wrongs. Love does not delight in evil but rejoices with the truth. It always protects, always trusts, always hopes, always perseveres." Emily and Michael knew that to build a Christ-centered marriage, they needed to embody these qualities in their relationship, loving each other selflessly, and putting the needs of their spouse above their own.

3. Shared Purpose

Emily and Michael were embarking on a journey together, and for it to be successful, they recognized the importance of a shared purpose. Their marriage was not just about them; it was about their commitment to serving God, their community, and each other. They acknowledged that by working together toward common goals, their love would flourish.

As Emily and Michael stepped out of the church into the bright future that awaited them, they carried with them the blueprint for their Christ-centered marriage. With faith in Christ, selfless love, and a shared purpose, they were equipped to face the challenges and joys that lay ahead. Their journey had just begun, and they were ready to build a love that would shine as a beacon of hope and inspiration to all who crossed their path.

2

The Cornerstone of Faith

Title: Building a Christ-Centered Marriage: A Blueprint for Love

In Chapter 1, we introduced the concept of a Christ-centered marriage as a blueprint for love. We explored the promise made by couples like Emily and Michael to base their union on the teachings of Christ, faith, selfless love, and shared purpose. In this chapter, we delve into the cornerstone of faith, the first pillar of their blueprint, and discover how it plays a vital role in constructing a strong, enduring Christ-centered marriage.

The Power of Faith

Faith serves as the bedrock upon which a Christ-centered marriage is built. Just as a building's foundation supports the entire structure, faith in Christ provides the unshakable support for the relationship. Emily and Michael understood that faith was not a passive element but an active force that needed nurturing and cultivation.

1. Faith in Christ's Teachings

For Emily and Michael, faith in Christ meant not only believing in His existence but also embracing His teachings. They recognized the importance of studying the Bible together, attending church regularly, and participating in spiritual growth opportunities as a couple. Through prayer and meditation on Christ's words, they sought to align their lives with His principles of love, forgiveness, and compassion.

2. Prayer as a Unifying Force

Prayer was an essential part of their daily routine. They understood that prayer was more than just a religious practice; it was a way to invite Christ into their marriage and seek His guidance. By praying together, Emily and Michael experienced unity, finding solace and strength in their shared moments of conversation with God.

3. Navigating Challenges Through Faith

In any marriage, challenges and conflicts are inevitable. Emily and Michael knew that their faith would be tested, but they had faith in their faith. They believed that their commitment to Christ would guide them through difficult times, helping them to forgive, heal, and grow stronger as a couple.

4. Attuning to God's Plan

A Christ-centered marriage requires couples to surrender their own desires to God's plan. This doesn't mean sacrificing personal aspirations, but it does mean being open to the direction God may have for their lives. Emily and Michael understood that God had a purpose for their marriage and were open to embracing it with faith and trust.

5. A Spiritual Support System

They actively sought out a community of like-minded individuals who could provide spiritual support and accountability. In their church family and close Christian friends, Emily and Michael found encouragement and mentorship that strengthened their faith and their marriage.

Faith, as the cornerstone of their Christ-centered marriage, provided Emily and Michael with unwavering support, guidance, and a shared sense of purpose. As they continued on their journey of love and devotion, they remained committed to deepening their faith in Christ, understanding that it was the source of their strength and the key to a lasting, thriving relationship. Their faith not only in God but also in each other was the essential building block that would enable them to construct a love that could withstand life's trials and tribulations.

3

Love in Action

Title: Building a Christ-Centered Marriage: A Blueprint for Love

In the previous chapters, we explored the foundational role of faith in a Christ-centered marriage. We discussed how faith in Christ provides unwavering support and guidance for couples like Emily and Michael. Now, in Chapter 3, we delve into the second pillar of their blueprint for love: selfless love in action.

The Call to Selfless Love

Selfless love is at the core of Christ's teachings, and it's a crucial element in building a Christ-centered marriage. Emily and Michael knew that to make their love more Christ-like, they had to actively practice selflessness in their daily lives.

1. Practicing Patience

Love is patient, and patience is an essential aspect of selfless love. Emily and Michael recognized that their partner, like themselves, was a work in progress. They chose to be patient, understanding that growth takes time and that their love would be fortified by their willingness to wait and support each other.

2. Acts of Kindness

Kindness is another manifestation of selfless love. Simple acts of kindness, like preparing a surprise meal or leaving love notes, became a regular part of their relationship. These actions helped nurture a loving, caring atmosphere within their home.

3. Forgiveness and Grace

In a Christ-centered marriage, forgiveness is not an option; it's a necessity. Emily and Michael understood the importance of forgiving each other for their shortcomings and mistakes, just as Christ forgives us. They also extended grace to one another, recognizing that they were both imperfect beings on a journey of growth.

4. Communication and Active Listening

Open, honest communication is essential for selfless love to flourish. Emily and Michael made a commitment to communicate effectively, listening to each other's thoughts, concerns, and dreams. By fostering an environment where both partners felt heard and valued, they nurtured a deeper bond of understanding.

5. Putting Each Other First

Selfless love means consistently prioritizing your partner's needs and well-being above your own. Emily and Michael learned to put each other's happiness and comfort before their own desires. They found joy in making sacrifices for the benefit of their relationship.

6. Serving Together

Serving others as a couple was an integral part of their marriage. They volunteered together at their church and in their community, allowing their shared purpose to strengthen their love. Through service, they not only grew individually but also as a couple.

7. The Power of Empathy

Empathy, the ability to understand and share in each other's feelings, was a powerful tool in their selfless love journey. By being empathetic, Emily and Michael could better support each other through life's challenges and celebrations.

8. Gratitude and Celebration

Being grateful for each other and the blessings in their life was a constant practice for Emily and Michael. They celebrated not just their milestones but also the small victories, finding joy in the everyday moments that made their love special.

In their quest to build a Christ-centered marriage, Emily and Michael recognized that selfless love was not a mere feeling but a commitment to actively love, cherish, and support one another. Their love in action was not just a reflection of Christ's love for them, but it also enriched their own lives, creating a fulfilling and joyful marriage. Through their unwavering dedication to selfless love, they learned that love was not just a noun but a verb – an ongoing, active, and transformative force that bound them together in a bond of unity, faith, and love.

4

A Shared Purpose

Title: Building a Christ-Centered Marriage: A Blueprint for Love

In the previous chapters, we explored the foundational role of faith and the essential practice of selfless love in a Christ-centered marriage. Now, in Chapter 4, we delve into the third and final pillar of the blueprint: the power of a shared purpose.

The Significance of Shared Purpose

A shared purpose in a Christ-centered marriage is the driving force that propels a couple toward common goals. Emily and Michael understood that having a clear direction and mission for their marriage was essential for their love to flourish.

1. Building a Family

Emily and Michael wanted to create a loving, Christ-centered family. This shared purpose guided their decisions regarding family planning, parenting, and fostering an environment where their children could grow in faith and love.

2. Serving the Community

They shared a commitment to serve their community as an extension of their faith. Volunteering together at church events, helping those in need, and participating in charitable activities were a significant part of their shared purpose.

3. Pursuing Individual Goals Together

Emily and Michael acknowledged that they were two individuals with unique dreams and aspirations. Their shared purpose was not about suppressing individual desires but finding ways to support each other in reaching personal goals, thereby enriching their partnership.

4. Nurturing Spiritual Growth

A key aspect of their shared purpose was the pursuit of spiritual growth. They attended Bible study groups, spiritual retreats, and other faith-based activities that allowed them to deepen their relationship with God as a couple.

5. Long-Term Goals and Planning

In their shared purpose, Emily and Michael set long-term goals for their marriage, such as financial stability, retirement planning, and creating a legacy of faith for their future generations.

6. Celebrating Milestones and Traditions

Establishing traditions and celebrating milestones were essential for creating lasting memories. They celebrated anniversaries, holidays, and other special occasions with rituals that strengthened their bond and reflected their shared purpose.

7. Facing Challenges Together

Their shared purpose was also a source of strength during difficult times. It provided them with a reason to persevere through challenges and a sense of unity that helped them overcome obstacles as a team.

8. Reinforcing Commitment

The shared purpose served as a reminder of their commitment to each other and to God. It anchored their marriage, reinforcing the importance of building their relationship on a foundation of faith and selfless love.

Emily and Michael's shared purpose not only gave their marriage direction but also added depth and meaning to their journey. Their shared goals and mission allowed them to grow and evolve as a couple, fostering unity, trust, and a deep connection that was grounded in their faith and love.

As we continue to explore the blueprint for a Christ-centered marriage, it becomes evident that faith, selfless love, and a shared purpose are interwoven threads that create a strong and resilient fabric. These pillars provide the strength and structure needed to build a love that endures and thrives, mirroring the love of Christ and serving as a source of inspiration for others. Emily and Michael's story reminds us that by embracing these principles, we too can embark on a path to building a Christ-centered marriage that is both timeless and transformative.

5

Nurturing the Garden of Love

Title: Building a Christ-Centered Marriage: A Blueprint for Love

In the preceding chapters, we've explored the essential pillars of faith, selfless love, and shared purpose in the blueprint for a Christ-centered marriage, using Emily and Michael's journey as our guide. Now, in Chapter 5, we delve into the ongoing commitment required to nurture the garden of love in such a marriage.

The Garden of Love

A marriage, like a garden, requires consistent care and attention. Emily and Michael understood that the love they had built would continue to grow and flourish only if they tended to it with love, diligence, and commitment.

1. Continuous Spiritual Growth

Their faith was not static; it was ever-evolving. They made a commitment to support each other's spiritual growth, encouraging one another to study the Bible, attend church, and engage in faith-building activities. They believed that as their individual relationships with Christ deepened, so would their shared spiritual connection.

2. Regular Self-Reflection

Selflessness meant taking the time to examine their own hearts and actions. Emily and Michael set aside moments for self-reflection, asking themselves if they were living in accordance with their commitment to selfless love. They acknowledged their imperfections and strived to improve.

3. Keeping the Romance Alive

While selflessness was central to their marriage, they also recognized the importance of nurturing the romantic aspect of their relationship. They prioritized date nights, thoughtful gestures, and expressions of love to keep the flames of romance burning.

4. Effective Communication

They continuously honed their communication skills. They worked on being active listeners, effectively expressing their needs and concerns, and ensuring that misunderstandings were addressed promptly. This commitment to open, honest communication helped to maintain a strong connection.

5. Embracing Change Together

Over the years, Emily and Michael knew they would face various changes – job transitions, family dynamics, health issues, and more. They committed to facing these changes together, adapting as a couple to the evolving circumstances of life.

6. Family Growth and Adaptation

With children and an expanding family, they acknowledged the need to adapt their shared purpose and their roles as parents. They continued to prioritize raising their children in a Christ-centered environment.

7. Seeking Guidance

They were not afraid to seek guidance when needed. They knew that, at times, they might require counsel from mentors, pastors, or therapists to navigate challenging times. They had faith that seeking help was a sign of strength, not weakness.

8. Revisiting the Blueprint

Finally, they understood that the blueprint for their marriage was not static. It required revisiting and refreshing as the years went by. They periodically reviewed their faith, love, and shared purpose, making adjustments as necessary.

Through this ongoing care and nurturing of their marriage, Emily and Michael found that their love grew stronger with each passing day. They recognized that love was not a one-time commitment but a continuous journey. Their Christ-centered marriage was a living testament to the transformative power of faith, selfless love, and shared purpose, which, when nurtured, allowed their love to blossom and thrive.

As we conclude this chapter and our exploration of the blueprint for a Christ-centered marriage, we are reminded that love is not a destination but a lifelong journey. The love Emily and Michael shared was a living example of what it means to build a love that endures, enriches, and radiates the grace of Christ. In the pages of their story, we find inspiration and guidance to embark on our own journey of love and faith, nurturing the garden of love for a lifetime.

6

Weathering Life's Storms

Title: Building a Christ-Centered Marriage: A Blueprint for Love

In the previous chapters, we've explored the vital components of faith, selfless love, shared purpose, and nurturing love in a Christ-centered marriage, using Emily and Michael's story as a guiding light. Now, in Chapter 6, we turn our attention to the inevitable challenges and storms that life may bring and how a Christ-centered marriage weathers them.

The Storms of Life

Marriage is not exempt from trials and tribulations; it's often in the midst of these storms that a couple's commitment to their faith, love, and shared purpose is tested.

1. Faith During Difficult Times

Emily and Michael knew that during challenging moments, faith was their anchor. They faced financial struggles, health issues, and personal setbacks, but they leaned on their faith in Christ for strength and resilience. Their unwavering belief in God's plan and purpose saw them through even the darkest of storms.

2. Selfless Love in Times of Adversity

During adversity, selfless love was their guiding light. They supported each other through personal crises, offering a shoulder to lean on and a listening ear. Their love was not conditional, but a constant source of support.

3. Unity in the Face of Challenges

Challenges could either divide a couple or bring them closer together. Emily and Michael chose unity. They faced challenges as a team, always reminding themselves of their shared purpose and the strength of their commitment to each other and to God.

4. Turning to Prayer and Reflection

In times of crisis, they turned to prayer and reflection. They prayed together, seeking God's wisdom and guidance. Self-reflection allowed them to learn from adversity and grow as individuals and as a couple.

5. Learning and Growing

They embraced adversity as an opportunity for personal and spiritual growth. Emily and Michael saw their struggles as refining fires that strengthened their faith and love. They believed that in God's grand design, even pain and suffering had a purpose.

6. Seeking Support from Others

Emily and Michael understood the importance of seeking support from their community and mentors during storms. They were not too proud to ask for help or guidance when needed. Their church family and close friends were a vital source of comfort and encouragement.

7. Forgiveness and Healing

During times of crisis, they also recognized the need for forgiveness and healing. Forgiving each other for the hurt and misunderstandings that might arise in times of stress was a cornerstone of their love. They understood that healing and restoration were possible with God's grace.

8. Remaining Steadfast

Their unwavering commitment to their blueprint for a Christ-centered marriage saw them through every storm. They never lost sight of their faith, selfless love, and shared purpose, even when the challenges felt insurmountable.

Emily and Michael's story serves as a testament to the resilience and strength of a Christ-centered marriage when faced with life's storms. Their journey teaches us that storms can be opportunities for growth, deepening love, and unwavering faith in God's plan. With faith as their anchor and selfless love as their guiding light, they found a way to weather life's adversities, ultimately emerging stronger and more closely knit as a couple.

As we conclude this chapter and our exploration of the blueprint for a Christ-centered marriage, we are reminded that it's not a question of if storms will come but when. A Christ-centered marriage provides a sturdy shelter during these storms, a refuge of love and faith that can withstand life's challenges. In the story of Emily and Michael, we find the inspiration to face adversity with grace and fortitude, knowing that a love founded on faith, selflessness, and shared purpose can indeed weather any storm.

7

An Ever-Deepening Love

Title: Building a Christ-Centered Marriage: A Blueprint for Love

In the previous chapters, we've explored the components of faith, selfless love, shared purpose, and the resilience needed to navigate life's storms in a Christ-centered marriage, as exemplified by the journey of Emily and Michael. In Chapter 7, we delve into the profound concept of an ever-deepening love that continues to grow and flourish with the passage of time.

The Journey of Love

The love of Emily and Michael wasn't static; it was a dynamic force that evolved and deepened as they journeyed together through the various stages of life.

1. A Deeper Connection with God

Their individual relationships with Christ continued to mature, which, in turn, deepened their shared connection with God. This spiritual growth allowed them to experience a profound sense of unity and intimacy in their marriage.

2. Discovering New Dimensions of Selfless Love

As their love deepened, they uncovered new facets of selfless love. Their commitment to putting each other first continued to evolve, and they found that selflessness was an ever-expanding reservoir of care and compassion.

3. An Enriched Shared Purpose

Over time, Emily and Michael's shared purpose expanded to encompass new aspirations and dreams. Their vision for their marriage grew in scope, becoming a powerful source of motivation and unity.

4. A Love that Withstands the Test of Time

Their enduring love was a testament to the strength of a Christ-centered marriage. Through the years, they continued to weather life's storms, remaining steadfast in their faith, selfless love, and shared purpose.

5. Deepening Intimacy

Their physical and emotional intimacy deepened with time. They learned to communicate more openly and understand each other on a deeper level. This intimacy was a natural outgrowth of their love and faith.

6. Shared Wisdom and Growth

As they grew older, they embraced the wisdom that comes with experience. They mentored younger couples and found joy in guiding others toward the blueprint they had embraced.

7. Facing Loss and Grief

Throughout their journey, Emily and Michael also faced loss and grief, but their faith and love allowed them to navigate these painful experiences with grace and hope.

8. Celebrating Milestones

They celebrated not only the big milestones but also the everyday moments of joy and triumph. These celebrations were a testament to the enduring strength of their love.

Emily and Michael's love deepened with each passing day, illustrating that a Christ-centered marriage is not a static entity but a living, breathing testament to the transformative power of faith and love. Their story serves as a reminder that as we nurture our faith, practice selfless love, and uphold a shared purpose, we create the conditions for love to continue growing and evolving, deepening with time, and ultimately, shining as a beacon of hope and inspiration to others.

As we conclude this chapter and our exploration of a Christ-centered marriage, we find that the blueprint for love is an ongoing process, a journey of growth and transformation. Through faith, selfless love, shared purpose, and the unwavering commitment to each other, we can build a love that not only stands the test of time but also continues to deepen and flourish, mirroring the boundless love and grace of Christ.

8

A Legacy of Love

Title: Building a Christ-Centered Marriage: A Blueprint for Love

In the previous chapters, we've explored the journey of Emily and Michael, who built their Christ-centered marriage based on faith, selfless love, shared purpose, resilience through life's challenges, and an ever-deepening love. Now, in Chapter 8, we examine the legacy of love they leave behind and how their blueprint for a Christ-centered marriage continues to inspire and impact the lives of those around them.

The Power of Legacy

A Christ-centered marriage is not just a personal journey but a legacy that can transform the lives of generations to come. Emily and Michael recognized the profound impact they could have on their family, friends, and community.

1. A Family Rooted in Faith

Their children grew up in an environment steeped in faith. Their Christ-centered marriage served as a model for the values and principles that would guide their own relationships and marriages.

2. Teaching by Example

Through their actions and the way they loved one another, Emily and Michael taught their children the significance of faith, selfless love, and shared purpose. Their children saw the beauty of a marriage grounded in Christ.

3. A Support System for Others

As a couple, they became a support system for friends and family facing marital challenges. Their blueprint for love became a source of wisdom, encouragement, and inspiration for others in their community.

4. Mentoring Young Couples

Emily and Michael actively mentored young couples who sought guidance in building Christ-centered marriages. They shared the lessons they had learned and encouraged others to embrace the same principles of faith, selfless love, shared purpose, and resilience.

5. Leaving a Testament of Love

Through their enduring love, they left a testament to the transformative power of Christ-centered love. Their legacy was a living example of the beauty that emerges when two people choose to build their marriage on a foundation of faith and selflessness.

6. Passing Down Traditions

They passed down traditions and rituals that reinforced their commitment to faith, selfless love, and shared purpose. These traditions continued to shape their family's values and sense of unity.

7. Leaving a Mark on the Community

Their involvement in their community, church, and charitable organizations had a lasting impact. The ripple effect of their love and service extended far beyond their immediate family.

8. A Marriage that Transcends Time

Emily and Michael's love was not bound by time. It continued to inspire, encourage, and uplift those who encountered their story, serving as a testament to the enduring nature of a Christ-centered marriage.

Emily and Michael's legacy was a testament to the enduring power of a Christ-centered marriage. They left a trail of love, wisdom, and inspiration that touched the lives of everyone they encountered. Their story illustrates that a Christ-centered marriage is not just about the love between two people but also the love they share with the world, leaving an indelible mark that continues to inspire and transform lives.

As we conclude our exploration of the blueprint for a Christ-centered marriage in this chapter, we find that a love founded on faith, selflessness, shared purpose, and resilience is not just a gift to the couple but a legacy that endures, enriches, and radiates the grace of Christ to all who are touched by it. Emily and Michael's journey serves as a reminder that through unwavering faith and selfless love, we can build a love that transcends time and continues to impact the world, leaving a lasting legacy of Christ-centered love.

9

Embracing the Journey

Title: Building a Christ-Centered Marriage: A Blueprint for Love

In the previous chapters, we've followed the remarkable journey of Emily and Michael as they built their Christ-centered marriage, embracing the components of faith, selfless love, shared purpose, resilience through life's challenges, and an ever-deepening love. Now, in Chapter 9, we explore the beauty of embracing the ongoing journey of a Christ-centered marriage and the enduring commitment that sustains it.

The Eternal Journey of Love

A Christ-centered marriage is not defined by a destination but by the journey itself. Emily and Michael recognized that their love would continue to evolve, deepen, and transform as they walked hand in hand in faith.

1. Embracing the Unknown

They embraced the unknown with open hearts and minds, understanding that life would bring both joy and adversity. Their faith in Christ gave them the strength to face whatever lay ahead.

2. Celebrating Anniversaries

Each anniversary was a testament to the love they had built and the commitment they had upheld. They celebrated these milestones as a couple, acknowledging the beauty of their shared journey.

3. Leaving a Mark in Their Wake

They continued to leave a mark on their family and community, offering guidance and support to others who were on their own journeys of faith and love.

4. Grateful Hearts

Emily and Michael never took their love for granted. They approached each day with gratitude for the gift of their Christ-centered marriage, knowing that it was a source of immense blessing.

5. A Lifelong Covenant

Their commitment to each other and to Christ was a covenant that remained unbroken. They understood that their love was a reflection of Christ's enduring love for them.

6. Inspiring the Next Generation

Their children and those they mentored continued to be inspired by the blueprint of love they had embraced. The legacy of their Christ-centered marriage was a beacon of hope for future generations.

7. Adapting and Growing

As they aged, they continued to adapt to the changes life brought their way.

Their shared purpose evolved, reflecting the evolving needs of their family and community.

8. A Love That Lives On

The love they had built was not confined to their own lifetimes. It lived on in the hearts of those they had touched, an eternal testament to the power of Christ-centered love.

Emily and Michael's story reminds us that a Christ-centered marriage is a journey, not a destination. It's a love that continues to transform, deepen, and inspire. Their journey underscores the idea that through faith, selfless love, shared purpose, resilience, and an enduring commitment, we can embark on a lifelong adventure of love, faith, and shared purpose.

In concluding this chapter, we find that a Christ-centered marriage is a living testament to the enduring and transformative power of faith and love. The journey may be marked by joys and challenges, but with faith as the compass, selfless love as the guiding star, and a shared purpose as the destination, a Christ-centered marriage becomes a radiant and ever-evolving love story that continues to shine, inspire, and endure for generations to come.

10

A Legacy of Love Continues

Title: Building a Christ-Centered Marriage: A Blueprint for Love

In the previous chapters, we've explored the extraordinary journey of Emily and Michael as they built their Christ-centered marriage, delving into faith, selfless love, shared purpose, resilience in the face of life's trials, and the enduring growth of love. Now, in Chapter 10, we contemplate the profound idea that the legacy of their love not only continues but also thrives, as the principles they lived by find new life in the hearts of those they've touched.

The Everlasting Impact of Love

Emily and Michael's legacy of love continues to unfold and create ripples of transformation, even after their earthly journey ends.

1. Transcending Time and Space

Their legacy exists beyond the confines of time and space. The love they shared, rooted in faith and selfless love, continues to inspire and transform the lives of generations that follow.

2. The Next Generation Carries the Torch

Their children, grandchildren, and great-grandchildren carry the torch of their Christ-centered love, passing on the values and principles that were the cornerstone of their enduring marriage.

3. An Inspiration for Others

The legacy of Emily and Michael's love serves as an inspiration for countless others who are on their own paths to building Christ-centered marriages. The lessons they imparted continue to guide couples on their journeys of faith and love.

4. Living a Testament to Christ's Love

Their story is a living testament to the boundless love and grace of Christ. It's a reminder that love, when rooted in faith, selflessness, and a shared purpose, is a force that endures, transcending all challenges and obstacles.

5. A Ripple Effect of Service

The legacy of their love extends to the community they served and the lives they touched. The selfless acts of kindness they performed continue to inspire others to serve their communities with love and dedication.

6. Celebrating Their Journey

Annually, their family and friends gather to celebrate the enduring legacy of Emily and Michael's love. These celebrations are a reminder of the beautiful journey of faith and selfless love that they undertook.

7. The Love That Never Fades

Their love is not forgotten or replaced but lives on in the hearts of those who remember them. It continues to enrich lives, uplift spirits, and spread the message of hope and faith.

8. An Eternal Love Story

Emily and Michael's love story is not just a chapter in their family's history; it's an eternal love story that transcends all boundaries and limitations.

The legacy of their love is a testament to the enduring power of faith and selfless love, and a reminder that love, when rooted in Christ, is a force that knows no bounds. It's a love that creates a legacy of hope, inspiration, and transformation, leaving a profound impact on those who have had the privilege of being touched by it.

As we conclude this final chapter of our exploration of the blueprint for a Christ-centered marriage, we find that the legacy of love is not just a reflection of the couple's journey but an eternal testament to the transformative power of faith, selflessness, and shared purpose. The legacy continues, reminding us that a Christ-centered marriage isn't just about the love between two individuals but a legacy that shines, inspires, and endures, like a beacon of Christ's love in this world and beyond.

11

Passing the Torch of Faith and Love

Title: Building a Christ-Centered Marriage: A Blueprint for Love

In the previous chapters, we've followed the incredible journey of Emily and Michael as they built their Christ-centered marriage, exploring the components of faith, selfless love, shared purpose, resilience in the face of life's trials, an ever-deepening love, and the legacy of love they left behind. Now, in Chapter 11, we reflect on how they pass the torch of faith and love to the next generation and continue to inspire the world.

The Flame of Faith and Love

Emily and Michael's enduring love story serves as a radiant torch, lighting the path for future generations to follow.

1. Teaching by Example

Their children and grandchildren have witnessed the transformative power of faith and selfless love in action. Emily and Michael's love wasn't just something they talked about; it was something they lived, and they passed down the invaluable lessons they had learned through their actions.

2. Embracing the Blueprint

The torch of their faith and love has been passed to the next generation. Inspired by their example, many of their descendants have embraced the blueprint for a Christ-centered marriage.

3. Guiding Young Couples

Their family is committed to mentoring young couples, just as Emily and Michael once did. They continue to be a source of wisdom and encouragement for those who seek to build Christ-centered marriages.

4. A Testament to Endurance

Emily and Michael's love story is a reminder that enduring faith and selfless love can withstand the tests of time and continue to inspire.

5. A Community Legacy

Their impact extends beyond their family. The community they served and the friends they touched continue to uphold the principles of faith and selfless love, which they so steadfastly demonstrated.

6. A Journey of Continual Growth

Emily and Michael's journey is not a story of static love, but a narrative of continuous growth and transformation. Their legacy lives on as their family members and mentees further deepen their own Christ-centered marriages.

7. An Enduring Flame

The torch of faith and love that Emily and Michael carried still burns brightly. It's a symbol of unwavering commitment to the blueprint they held dear, a legacy that thrives with each new day.

8. A Testament to Christ's Love

Emily and Michael's love story is, at its core, a testament to the love of Christ. It radiates the boundless grace and compassion that Christ offers, a gift that is passed down through the generations.

Emily and Michael's legacy is a testament to the power of Christ-centered love to inspire, uplift, and transform. Their journey is an eternal reminder that faith and selfless love are not just guiding principles but living forces that have the ability to touch the lives of generations to come.

As we conclude this chapter, we are reminded that the torch of faith and love, ignited by Emily and Michael, continues to burn brightly, guiding future generations toward the transformative power of faith, selflessness, and shared purpose. Their legacy is a lasting testament to the blueprint for a Christ-centered marriage and a radiant beacon of Christ's love that continues to inspire the world.

12

The Ongoing Story of Love

Title: Building a Christ-Centered Marriage: A Blueprint for Love

In the preceding chapters, we have embarked on a journey with Emily and Michael as they built their Christ-centered marriage, exploring the integral components of faith, selfless love, shared purpose, resilience through life's trials, an ever-deepening love, and the legacy of love they've left behind. Now, in Chapter 12, we reflect on the ever-evolving and enduring story of their love as it continues to inspire and shape the lives of those who have followed in their footsteps.

The Unfolding Love Story

Emily and Michael's love story is not a chapter that ends but a narrative that continues to evolve and inspire.

1. A Source of Hope

Their love story remains a source of hope and inspiration, touching the hearts of those who have encountered it. It reminds us that a Christ-centered marriage is a blueprint for a love that knows no bounds.

2. Celebrating Their Journey

Annually, their family and friends gather to celebrate the enduring legacy of Emily and Michael's love. These celebrations are a reminder of the beautiful journey of faith and selfless love that they undertook.

3. A Testament to Christ's Love

Their story is a living testament to the boundless love and grace of Christ. It's a reminder that love, when rooted in faith, selflessness, and shared purpose, is a force that endures, transcending all challenges and obstacles.

4. Passing the Torch

The torch of their faith and love has been passed on to the next generation. Inspired by their example, many of their descendants have embraced the blueprint for a Christ-centered marriage.

5. A Living Legacy

Emily and Michael's legacy lives on in the hearts of those who continue to practice the principles of faith and selfless love that they held dear. It's a testament to the enduring impact of a Christ-centered love story.

6. The Power of a Christ-Centered Marriage

Their story illustrates that a Christ-centered marriage is not just about the love between two people but a legacy that shines, inspires, and endures, like a beacon of Christ's love in this world and beyond.

7. A Love that Continues to Grow

Emily and Michael's love story reminds us that love is not static. It continues to grow, deepen, and inspire, providing hope and encouragement to those who are on their own journeys of faith and love.

8. A Testament to Faith and Love

Their journey serves as a testament to the transformative power of faith and selfless love. It demonstrates that through unwavering commitment to each other and to God, we can build a love that not only stands the test of time but continues to deepen and flourish.

As we conclude this chapter and our exploration of the blueprint for a Christ-centered marriage, we find that a love founded on faith, selflessness, shared purpose, resilience, and an enduring commitment is not just a gift to the couple but a legacy that endures, enriches, and radiates the grace of Christ. Emily and Michael's love story reminds us that through the unwavering faith and selfless love they practiced, we can build a love that transcends time, offering hope and inspiration to all who encounter it.

Their ongoing story of love serves as a living testament to the enduring and transformative power of faith and love. It is a reminder that a Christ-centered marriage is not just a destination but an ever-evolving journey, a narrative of love and faith that continues to inspire and shape the lives of generations to come.

Book Summary: "Building a Christ-Centered Marriage: A Blueprint for Love"

"Building a Christ-Centered Marriage: A Blueprint for Love" is a heartwarming and inspiring journey that explores the transformative power of faith, selfless love, shared purpose, and enduring commitment within the context of a Christ-centered marriage. This book follows the remarkable story of Emily and Michael, a couple whose enduring love serves as a beacon of hope and guidance for couples seeking to build lasting, Christ-centered relationships.

The book is divided into twelve chapters, each addressing a unique facet of their journey:

Chapter 1: Foundation of Faith
In the opening chapter, we discover the pivotal role of faith in Emily and Michael's marriage. Their unwavering belief in Christ became the bedrock upon which they built their enduring love.

Chapter 2: Selfless Love
The second chapter delves into the concept of selfless love. Emily and Michael's love story underscores the significance of putting each other's needs before their own, creating a selfless love that is both transformative and enduring.

Chapter 3: A Shared Purpose
Chapter 3 explores the power of a shared purpose in a Christ-centered marriage. Emily and Michael's mission and goals provided them with direction and unity, strengthening their relationship.

Chapter 4: Nurturing the Garden of Love
In the fourth chapter, we learn how Emily and Michael cultivated their love like a garden, tending to it with care, diligence, and attention to both the spiritual and emotional dimensions of their relationship.

Chapter 5: Weathering Life's Storms
Chapter 5 details how they faced the trials and tribulations of life. Their unwavering faith and selfless love served as anchors during difficult times, highlighting the resilience required in a Christ-centered marriage.

Chapter 6: An Ever-Deepening Love
The sixth chapter explores how Emily and Michael's love evolved and deepened over time. Their commitment to faith and selflessness allowed their love to flourish and continue growing, even as they aged.

Chapter 7: A Legacy of Love

Chapter 7 illustrates the lasting legacy of their Christ-centered marriage. It extends beyond their own lives, impacting their family, community, and future generations, leaving a mark of love and faith.

Chapter 8: Embracing the Journey

In the eighth chapter, we're reminded that a Christ-centered marriage is not a destination but an ongoing journey. Emily and Michael embraced the unknown with open hearts and minds, celebrating each moment along the way.

Chapter 9: Passing the Torch of Faith and Love

Chapter 9 reflects on how their legacy of faith and love is passed to the next generation. Their children and mentees continue to uphold the principles of a Christ-centered marriage, carrying the torch forward.

Chapter 10: The Ongoing Story of Love

Chapter 10 contemplates the enduring and ever-evolving love story of Emily and Michael. Their love continues to inspire and shape the lives of those who follow in their footsteps.

Chapter 11: A Legacy of Love Continues

In this chapter, we observe the lasting impact of their love, illuminating the power of a Christ-centered marriage to inspire and uplift, touching hearts and enriching lives even after their journey on earth ends.

Chapter 12: The Eternal Journey of Love

The final chapter reflects on the timeless nature of their love story. Emily and Michael's love isn't bound by time but continues to flourish, inspire, and impact the world, just like the boundless love of Christ.

"Building a Christ-Centered Marriage: A Blueprint for Love" is a moving narrative that offers readers a blueprint for building strong, enduring, and deeply fulfilling Christ-centered marriages. Emily and Michael's story serves as a testament to the enduring and transformative power of faith, selfless love, shared purpose, and an unwavering commitment to one another and to Christ.

www.ingramcontent.com/pod-product-compliance
Lightning Source LLC
LaVergne TN
LVHW010439070526
838199LV00066B/6084